Preface: The Princess & Dragon Story

This collection of stories has a very

special meaning. It takes me back to

the early days of being a father with a

beautiful little girl sitting on my knee for story time.

Like all little girls, she loved stories about princesses

and dragons. She still does! This volume is dedicated

to her.

Of course, this collection isn't just for girls!

There are plenty of dragons, knights and other

adventures that boys will love. I know first-hand

because my boys (6 and 10) loved reading every story

before they were published.

It seems there is nothing more treasured in literature than the princess and dragon story. Why? Because children love adventure and danger, heroes and heroines, and of course, happy endings. Every story, every word, every adventure, every daring rescue, every lesson learned — it's all new and exciting to children.

Through these stories, they explore the world around them. They learn about good vs. evil, about friendship and love, about right and wrong, about choices and consequences and so much more.

And all the while, their inquisitive minds are learning new vocabulary, improving listening and reading skills, and literally being hard-wired to learn

- preparing them to become successful in school and

in life.

There is no better early childhood development

program than when a parent takes the time to sit

down and read with a child every day. To that end,

we offer you this special collection of timeless

princess and dragon stories in the hope that both you

and your child will love the experience of joining in

the adventures and excitement together.

Phillip J. Chipping // Founder
knowonder! publishing
www.knowonder.com

About DyslexiAssist™

Part of our mission at Knowonder! Publishing is to make literacy more effective. In order to fulfill that mission for children suffering from dyslexia we are proud to announce our new DyslexiAssist™ initiative: to publish each of our books in a special font designed to make reading easier for dyslexics. You can learn more about it on our website at:

www.knowonder.com/dyslexiassist

When reading with this new font, independent research shows that 84% of dyslexics read faster, 77% read with fewer mistakes, and 76% recommend the font to others who suffer from dyslexia.

But the magic isn't just in the font. We take

extra care to make the font an appropriate size, give

proper spacing to letters in the words, make sure that

there are the exact right number of words on each

line, and so much more! The layout of the book is just

as important. We go to extra lengths to make sure

all the stars are aligned so they, too, can know the

wonder of reading.

Reading stories is a highly enjoyable form of

entertainment but people with dyslexia have been

unable to find the same joy from books. We hope this

new initiative can now bring the same love and joy of

reading and learning to your home!

Table of Contents

A collection

of princess and dragon stories

(perfect for bedtime!)

for children ages 0-12

and for parents

who want to feel like a kid again.

- Volume 1 -

ISBN: 978-1517017095

Dedicated to my princess,

my "darling angel baby doll."

I love you forever!

Spread Your Wings

by Laird Long

Princess Suzy awoke, as she did every morning, with her pet dragon, Ollie, snuggled into her side next to her in bed. Ollie liked to burrow under the warm blankets of the large bed, pretending like he was in a cave. He softly snored, just a wisp of smoke trickling out of his mouth now and then, as the Princess contentedly sighed.

Suzy was a small girl for her age. Ollie was a small dragon for his age. They were always together; running and rolling about on the vast, lush, green lawns of the Royal Palace; dashing and jumping around in the huge, flower-perfumed gardens at the rear of the palace; splashing in and rowing on the large, lily pad-dappled lake that lay to the east of the palace; or romping through the towering green trees that spread out to the west in the Royal Forest.

This morning, like previous mornings, Princess Suzy blinked her big blue eyes and stared up at the high, oak-beamed ceiling of her bedroom. Then she yawned, stretched out her arms and legs, as she felt the warm little body of Ollie stir next to her. She raised her golden-blonde head up off the fluffy white pillow and threw back the royal red blankets on her bed, revealing the dozing green dragon.

"Rise and shine, Ollie!" she exclaimed as she always did.

The dragon's eyes popped open, then narrowed

into yellow slits with green hoods. He smacked his thin lips and coughed a little bit of smoke. Then he unfurled his neck and gazed up at Suzy, grinning as baby dragons grin. Finally, he rose unsteadily on his little legs and arched his green-scaled back, his tiny, membraned wings quivering.

Girl and dragon leapt out of bed and scampered over to the large dining and play table at the other end of the room. Suzy pulled out a chair and sat down. Ollie jumped into her lap, then onto the table and sat up.

"Good morning, my dears!" Nanny Katherine greeted the pair, right on schedule. She entered the bedroom carrying a silver tray. She set the tray down on the table and then placed a china bowl full of

oatmeal in front of Suzy along with a gold goblet of

orange juice and plunked down a silver dish of dragon

food in front of Ollie. Breakfast was served.

"So, what are you two planning to get up to

today?" Katherine asked, part of the daily ritual.

She watched the girl and the dragon happily dig into

their food. Nanny Katherine had been with the Royal

Family for years. She'd even raised Queen Millicent,

Suzy's mother, from a child.

"We're going to catch butterflies in the garden

this morning!" Suzy responded, gleefully gulping a

spoonful of oatmeal. "Aren't we, Ollie?"

Ollie lifted his head out of his bowl and eagerly

nodded. Then he licked his lips with a long, pink, forked tongue.

"That sounds like fun," Nanny Katherine agreed. "But didn't you two just do that a few days ago?"

Suzy giggled and shrugged. Ollie grinned and burped smoke, then ducked his head back down into his bowl.

After breakfast Princess Suzy had changed into her favorite white summer dress with the broad blue sash around her waist, and was skipping down the red-carpeted hallway that led to the Royal Terrace and gardens, when she heard someone crying. She hopped to a stop, jumped backwards, and peeked around the oaken doorway of one of the opulent rooms that lined the hallway.

"But I'm afraid she'll...never grow up!" Queen Millicent lamented to a man in black, standing uneasily in front of her.

Suzy recognized the man with her mother as the Royal Physician, Doctor Leopold.

"She hasn't gotten any bigger at all. She's still such a small child," the Queen said, tears glittering in her large blue eyes. "Why won't she grow up!?"

Doctor Leopold grimaced, both at the heartfelt anguish of his Monarch and at his own inability to properly and professionally address it. "I'm afraid I just don't know, your Majesty," he said. "Nor do the best medical minds in the Kingdom. I've consulted them all." He wrung his long, slender hands in frustration. "She should be a young lady by now. But obviously isn't. Perhaps...more time–"

"More time?" Queen Millicent wailed. "I'm an ill woman, doctor, as you know! I don't have much more time!" She looked down at her own pale, delicate hands writhing in despair in her lap, and the jewel-encrusted crown atop her blonde head slipped slightly. "Suzy should be experiencing all of the joys of young womanhood by now — learning, loving...growing!"

The Queen covered her face with her hands and sobbed. "Becoming a queen herself!"

Suzy gripped the edge of the doorway, her eyes gone wide, startled to hear her own name mentioned.

Doctor Leopold hung his head. Queen Millicent wept.

Princess Suzy walked slowly down the hallway, out onto the gleaming marble terrace of the palace, and down into the sprawling gardens where her little pet dragon, Ollie, was already frolicking about amongst the brightly-colored flowers and lush green plants, under a warm yellow sun.

The pair caught many beautiful butterflies. Suzy chased them with her white lace butterfly net, Ollie running along at her heels. As she swooped around with the net, he would jump up into the air, his tiny wings beating like he meant to fly. But, unlike the butterflies, he could never stay airborne for long.

Then they examined the winged insects they'd

captured up-close; studying the intricate polka-

dot and diamond and triangular patterns on the

butterflies' wings, marveling at the brilliant blue and

orange and purple hues before setting the butterflies

free again and watching them flutter away.

It was when they were watching a large Monarch

butterfly spread its bright orange and black wings and

fly away that they spotted the four dragons up in the

air not far off. They were young dragons, but bigger

than Ollie. And they were obviously just learning to

fly, flapping their wings furiously to stay in the air.

But as they quickly gained confidence and

spread their wings, they began soaring and swooping,

playfully sailing through the soft blue sky, the flares

of flame from their open mouths revealing their joy.

Suzy glanced down at Ollie on the ground. The

little dragon's eyes were wide and shining, darting

about with the exhilarating movements of the other

dragons flying in the sky. His small green body

twitched with excitement, his limbs trembling, his tiny

wings beating frantically and futilely. He just didn't

have the size and strength to get off the ground,

though he obviously wanted to.

It was in a dragon's nature to fly, after all. Just

as it was in a princess' nature to grow up to become

a Queen.

Princess Suzy confronted Nanny Katherine that

afternoon as they shared tea and sandwiches at

a small wicker table down by the lake. Ollie was

flopped out flat on his green belly on the green grass

next to Suzy's chair, snoozing and soaking up the

sun.

"I want you to let Ollie grow bigger," Suzy

stated, setting down her Royal Crest-emblazoned

china teacup. "I don't think it's right to keep him so

small anymore."

Katherine briefly choked on her tomato and

lettuce sandwich. "But that's what you wanted me to

do! Ordered me to do!" she protested.

Suzy looked down at the dozing little dragon. "I

know. I didn't want Ollie to grow up into a big, flying,

fire-breathing dragon that would have to be put out

of the palace one day and leave me. I wanted him to

stay small and cute and always be my companion."

She blinked her big blue eyes and her dimpled

chin quivered. "But that was wrong. I know that now.

Getting you to use your magical powers to change...

nature."

Princess Suzy lifted her golden-blonde head and

looked firmly at Nanny Katherine. "And I want you

to let me grow up, as well. I've been a little girl,

someone for you to play with and look after too

long."

Katherine desperately shook her head. "Oh no,

Princess Suzy! I would never do that!"

Suzy reached out her little hand across the table and grasped one of Katherine's weathered hands. She spoke with a compassion and confidence beyond her size. "I heard Mother talking to Doctor Leopold — about me. I know you did it, Nanny. And...I don't blame you. I put the idea into your head, after all, with Ollie."

Katherine gazed lovingly at the Princess. "You're such a beautiful little girl. Just like your mother was. And she grew up and left my care, and now she's ill. I didn't want the same thing to happen you." She smiled, tears trickling down her wrinkled cheeks.

Suzy smiled back, squeezing Katherine's hand. "We all have to grow up." She looked down at the sleeping dragon. "Otherwise we'll never be able to spread our wings and fly."

Nanny Katherine ended up living long enough to attend the Royal Wedding. She and the other hundreds of guests watched in awe as a giant green dragon flapped its tremendous wings and swooped down out of a soft blue sky with Queen Susan upon its back.

Susan's golden-blonde hair shone under the warm yellow sun as the young woman slid off Oliver's back, radiant in the white lace wedding dress her mother had once worn. She smiled at Nanny Katherine and patted Oliver on the head.

And then the old woman wept with joy, and the

young dragon tilted its head up and breathed out

a celebratory stream of fire as the Queen took the

hand of her beloved, and a firm grasp on her future.

the end.

The Princess Who Would Not Eat

by Ann Burnett

"I don't care," said the princess.

"If you don't eat, you won't grow up into a big strong princess," said her pop the king.

"I don't want to be a big strong princess." Nothing would convince her to eat. Her parents stopped her pocket money, put her to bed without any tea, (she didn't mind that) and even kept her inside (she did mind that). But still she did not eat.

One Sunday, the queen called for her chief chef. "Chief chef, can you make a dish that the princess will eat?"

"Most certainly, Queen," said the chief chef. "Right away." He worked in the kitchens all day and then presented the dish to the queen. "French fries, slaw, and wieners covered in tomato ketchup," he

said. The queen showed it to the princess.

"Yuck," she said. "I'm not eating that." And she

threw it over the chief chef.

On Monday, the chief chef tried again. "Ice

cream, chocolate sauce, raspberries, and cherries," he

announced, offering the dish to the princess.

"Pooh!" said the princess. "I don't like that."

And she pushed the chief chef's face into it.

On Tuesday, the chief chef was very busy.

"Custard and hamburgers with rhubarb and cheese

sauce," he said. The princess sniffed at it.

"Hmmm," she said. She took a mouthful and spat

it out. "It tastes horrible!" she yelled and threw it

to the royal cat.

On Wednesday, the chief chef was looking worried. At last, he marched up the stairs from the kitchens with a large dish. "Fish heads with orange Jell-O, peanut butter, and teabags."

"Do try some dear," said the queen. "It looks... delicious."

The princess poked it with her finger. "It smells dreadful," she said and put it on her pop's throne. Squelch! went the king when he sat down.

Thursday was a busy day in the kitchens. All sorts of cooking smells wafted up through the palace.

"Roast beef," sniffed a maid.

"Treacle pudding," said a footman.

"Meaty bones," snuffled Rex the king's dog.

"Salmon soufflé," purred the royal cat.

At last, the chief chef came out with his latest dish. "Tutti-frutti ice cream with marshmallows, meringues, and marzipan mayonnaise," he said, feeling very pleased.

"That looks scrumptious," said the king, helping himself to a spoonful.

"You can have it then," said the princess. "I'm not eating that."

The king ate every mouthful of it and then he was sick.

"Serves you right for being greedy," said the princess. "I'm glad I didn't eat any."

"I think it was a bit rich," the queen told the chief chef. "Something simple for tomorrow."

On Friday, the chief chef read every recipe book he had. Then he read them again. He scratched his head and worried all day until he had no time left to cook. Quickly, he opened a can of tomato soup.

"Er, tomato soup," he said, setting it down in front of the princess.

"Is that all?" she yelled. "How boring! I'm not eating that!"

The chief chef took off his chief chef's hat. "I'm leaving," he said to the king and queen. "I've had enough."

"Don't go," begged the king. "What will we do?

Our daughter is getting thinner and thinner. How can we make her eat?"

"Send for Jack, the wisest man in the world," said the chief chef.

"Fetch him right away," ordered the queen.

On Saturday, Jack, the wisest man in the world, who was the chief chef's brother, was very busy when the messenger arrived.

"Oh, dear," he said when he heard the news. "I was going to cut my corn and milk my cows today." But Jack had to go to the palace instead.

"What do you want?" he asked the king and queen.

"Our daughter won't eat," they said. "Can you

help?"

Jack looked at the princess. She was sitting on her throne pulling the loose threads out and kicking the footstool. "I'm bored," she said. "There's nothing to do and nothing I want to eat. It's all boring."

"I know where the most delicious food in all the world is to be had," said Jack. "But only a few special people can eat it."

"Where's that?" asked the princess.

"I don't know if you will be able to get there," said Jack. "It's a long way."

"Of course I can do it," said the princess. "Let's go."

The princess set off with Jack. They walked for

miles and miles.

"Is it far now?" asked the princess.

"Yes," said Jack. "Very far. I told you it would

be." They walked on and on.

"I'm thirsty," said the princess. "And hungry. Can

I have something to eat?"

"Not until we reach the most delicious food in

the world," said Jack.

At last, they reached his cottage.

"First we must gather in the corn," said Jack.

The princess helped cut the corn and stack it in

heaps.

"I'm starving," said the princess. "Where is this

special food?"

"Be patient," said Jack. "We have to thresh the corn." The princess helped thresh the corn and then grind it into flour. She helped Jack mix the flour into dough and put it near the fire to rise.

"I'm absolutely ravenous," said the princess. "Where is this food?"

"Not yet," said Jack. "Now we have to milk the cows." The princess sat beside a cow and squeezed the milk into a bucket. When she had finished, she helped Jack pour the milk into a tub and add rennet to make cheese.

"I could eat a horse," said the princess. "Can we go and find this delicious food now?"

"Wait," said Jack, "we have to bake the bread."

The princess shaped the dough into loaves and put them in the oven. Soon a rich baking smell filled the cottage.

"Ooh," sighed the princess. "I've never smelt anything so wonderful before."

"We haven't finished yet," said Jack. "Fill the bucket from the well." The princess went to the well and lowered the bucket. When she pulled it up, the bucket was full of clear sparkling water. She carried it into the kitchen. Jack, the wisest man in the world, was sitting at the table with a fresh baked loaf of bread and the cheese he had made.

"Come and taste the most delicious food in the world," he said to the princess. The princess ate the bread and cheese and drank the water from the well.

She ate and ate and ate until there was not a crumb

left.

"You were right," said the princess. "That was

the most delicious food in the world! And I've been

so busy working, I haven't been bored all day."

"Would you like to come back and help me again

next Saturday?" Jack asked.

"Yes," the princess said with a smile. "As long as

I get to eat as much as I want when we're done!"

the end.

The Hedge Dragon

by Jonathan Kemmerer-Scovner

"I hear you like mazes, Your Majesty."

Nora's eyes widened at the old man who had crossed her path. "Oh, yes!" she answered. She was just fifteen years old, but everyone in the kingdom knew how much she loved them. It was hardly a birthday if there weren't a dozen woodworkers eager to present their finest mazes to the King's only daughter.

"That being the case," continued the old man, "I have something you might enjoy."

Intrigued, Nora followed. All about her, the countryside was filled with artisans and bakers selling their wares, bolts of fabric, and hand-stitched books. She'd been wandering the festival grounds for some time but so far had found nothing of interest.

At last they came to a hill overlooking a valley. What she saw took her breath away. "It's... it's amazing!" she gasped.

Spread out before her was the largest hedge maze she'd ever seen—passages and dead-ends, hard angles and twisting turns, stretching as far as she could see!

"I've never seen this before! Where did this come from?"

"There's a touch of magic about it, if you must know. I have my very own Hedge Dragon!"

Nora gasped. "A real one?"

"We travel from kingdom to kingdom. He creates

the mazes and I drum up the business!"

"I've always wanted to meet a Hedge Dragon."

"Well, then. There's a surprise waiting for you in the center. If you can find it, that is."

So Princess Nora of the North Kingdom entered the old man's hedge maze, quickly disappearing around the first of its many bends.

"If you can find it," he repeated.

It was a most unusual maze. Several times she was certain she was headed in one direction, only to find herself back where she'd begun. When she turned back, she found herself somewhere different. A touch of magic, indeed! she thought to herself. Regardless, turn by turn, she slowly closed in on the center.

She knew she had to be quick. Mother would be worried if she didn't come back soon.

Finally, she came to a large, open area with a fountain. Beside it, Nora was startled to discover, rested a large, green dragon.

"Oh, hello there!" she called out. "Are you my surprise?"

"I suppose that depends on whether or not you're surprised," the dragon replied.

"You're the Hedge Dragon. The old man told me about you!" When the dragon did not respond, she asked, "Is something wrong?"

"That old man is a wizard. He stole me from my nest and has forced me to make the mazes for him ever since."

"That's silly!" Nora smiled. "Why would he do that?"

"So he can use them to trap people. Such as yourself, Princess."

"But I haven't been captured! I'm just..." Her smile faded as she noticed the hedge walls moving. "No!" In a moment, Nora was running through the shifting hedges, narrowly sliding through passages. "No one has yet made a maze that can trap me!" she muttered. She was certain she was just one more turn from freedom when she stumbled back into the center.

"Nice to see you again," said the dragon.

"This maze... it's not fair!" she panted. "A maze has a beginning and an end. That's the whole point!"

"The point?" The Hedge Dragon sat on its rear haunches. "The point of a maze is to trick. To deceive. To make you more lost than you've been before with no hope of ever being found!"

Nora crossed her arms. "You're a barrel of sunshine, aren't you?"

"I told you," said the Hedge Dragon as they stepped through the passages. "There's no way out. I create the mazes, but he casts his spell to make escape impossible."

"So why don't you just fly away? Or burn it down?"

"It's part of the spell. I can only escape if I find

my way out of the maze."

They came to an intersection. Nora turned right.

"And what is your interest in mazes, Princess?"

asked the beast as he followed.

"I've loved them ever since I can remember." They

came to another intersection at which Nora turned

left. "I made them out of pebbles I found in the

garden and made my dolls get lost in them. When the

other kids were making sandcastles, I was digging out

tidewater labyrinths."

"It is the same for us. We make them out of

rocks or trees or whatever we can find. Even the

babies will begin arranging the sticks in their nests to

form passages. We don't know why we do it. When we get older, we can create hedge mazes out of thin air. I hope someday I can escape and find out more about my kind."

"Yes, I could tell you were just dying to escape from the moment I saw you." Four paths branched out in separate directions. Nora asked, "Which way would you go?"

The Hedge Dragon craned his neck down each one. "Not that it matters, but this way," he said, selecting the center path.

The sun set over the hedges, and they were still nowhere near the end. "Maybe we should rest," said Nora.

The stars came out before long, cold and twinkling. Nora rested against the dragon's belly. "Do you ever try to connect the stars and make mazes out of them?" she asked. "My father got so angry when I marked up his star charts...What's wrong?"

The Hedge Dragon had covered his head and sobbed softly. "What good is a Hedge Dragon who can't find his way out of his own maze? It's like a groundhog not finding his way out of the earth, or a bird not finding its way out of the sky. My parents would be so ashamed!"

"I'm sure your parents would be proud. Especially after you tell them how you stood up to the wizard and escaped."

"You think so?"

"Yes, I..." Suddenly, she stopped. "Do you hear that?"

"The wizard captures other creatures in here as well," cautioned the dragon.

Suddenly, there appeared before them an army of tiny creatures wearing black armor. The tallest one didn't quite make it to Nora's knees.

"Who goes there?" asked the leader in a high-pitched voice.

"I am Nora, Princess of the North Kingdom. This is my friend, the Hedge Dragon."

"What?" The tiny warrior aimed his black sword at the beast. "You created this maze? Get him, men!"

The tiny soldiers raised their swords and shouted

in their high-pitched war-cries, "Attack!"

"Stop!" cried Nora. "It's not his fault! He's

under a spell by an evil wizard. He wants to escape

just like the rest of us!"

"Hm. Because you're a princess, I will believe

you." The captain of the army lowered his sword. "At

ease, men."

"At ease!" the tiny soldiers cried out.

"We are the Pinquots. An old man led us into

this maze, promising us a treasure at its center. That

was one week ago. We've been up and down every

way you can go, and now we're growing weak from

hunger."

"Let's camp together," Nora suggested.

"Tomorrow morning we'll figure out a way to escape,
I promise."

That night, Nora dreamed she was doing mazes in
her bedroom at home while her mother chided her for
not playing outside.

"You spend so much time by yourself," said the
Queen, not realizing that one of the things Nora liked
about mazes was the fact that she could do them
alone. "You need to learn how to work with other
people."

Nora awoke with a start. The sun was just coming
up. She saw the heap of snoozing Pinquots and the

long, red banners tied around their waists.

That's it! If we're going to get out of here, we'll have to work together!

Before long, she had awoken them all. "There are eight of you and two of us," she said. "That means we can split up into twos. When you reach a dead-end, turn back to the last intersection and tie a bit of your red banner to it. That way, we'll know which passages are dead ends."

"Just a minute!" said the leader of the Pinquots. "I'm in charge here!"

Nora breathed heavy. "I'm sorry."

"Men," he commanded. "Do what she says."

"Aye, sir!" shouted the Pinquots.

"But Princess!" said the Hedge Dragon. "You're forgetting that this maze is cursed. The passages keep changing!"

"If the passages wind back on each other, then we'll know not to go down them. And if a passage closes up, we'll just have to wait for it to open up again. There just has to be a way out."

The sun was on its way back down before they finished, and the hedge maze was filled with red fabric.

"It's working," said Nora. "I can feel it. We're getting near the...There!"

Before them, two hedges closed in on each other.

"I saw the exit!" she declared. "I'm certain of it!

We'll just have to wait for it to open up again."

"But what if it doesn't?" asked the Hedge Dragon.

"They open and close automatically. The wizard isn't controlling them, otherwise we wouldn't have made it this far. Get ready! When they open, we may not have much time!"

They waited for an hour. Then another hour.

"Princess Nora," said the Hedge Dragon.

"Yes?"

"I was thinking...perhaps when we escape, I could help you make a hedge maze for your castle. As a...a thank-you."

"When we escape?" Nora smiled. "That's the

first hopeful thing I've heard you say."

The dragon blushed. "Well..."

"Look!" cried the Pinquot captain.

Sure enough, the hedges had pulled back, and

there they all saw the exit.

"Charge!"

Eight Pinquots, a princess, and a Hedge Dragon

all stumbled and poured through the opening of the

maze, collapsing in a heap just outside of it.

"Are we all out? Did we make it?" Nora did a

quick head count, and sure enough, they were all

accounted for.

"Hoo-rah!" shouted the Pinquots.

"I've got to find my parents." said Nora. "I've

got to tell them..."

"Tell them what?"

It was a deep, bellowing voice, and it belonged

to the old man, who now stood tall and upright

with a black cape billowing in the breeze. He cast a

crooked finger at the Hedge Dragon. "Traitor! You

showed them how to escape. I ought to turn you into

topiary!"

The Hedge Dragon growled, and Nora called out,

"Don't touch my friend!"

"Or else what?"

At that, the Pinquots shouted, "Attack!" and

charged forward with their black swords at the ready.

The wizard fell to the earth in surprise, batting

them away, and in a moment, the dragon had lifted him in his mouth, far above the tallest Pinquot.

"I knew you'd come to your senses!" said the wizard, dangling upside down. "Now be a good boy and set me down."

With a flick of his mighty neck, the Hedge Dragon tossed the wizard over the wall of hedges so he landed within the maze.

"Get me out of here!" they heard the distant shout.

"Do you think he'll be able to find his way out?" asked Nora.

"Not a chance," said the Hedge Dragon with a wink.

The King and Queen were so happy to see their

daughter again. Sending in a battalion of knights,

they were able to capture the dark wizard — though

it took some time for them to get back out of the

maze.

The Pinauots returned to their native land,

pleased to have assisted in the rescue of the North

Kingdom's only princess.

And for her next birthday, Princess Nora invited

all of the children of the kingdom to play in the most

wondrous hedge maze they'd ever seen, right there in

the castle courtyard, and what a surprise they had

when they reached the center!

The End.

The Dragon Tree

by Rolli

I was eating blueberries with my dragon. My dragon is a fussy eater. He only likes blueberries that are perfectly round and sweet. If they're not sweet, he spits them out. "That's wasting," I told him. But my dragon didn't care. He just shrugged his wings and pointed at the berries I spat out. Then I told my dragon, "Be quiet."

When we ran out of blueberries, we moved on to strawberries. There's a strawberry patch in the forest by my house. They're wild strawberries so we have to be quiet. Wild strawberries are shy.

My dragon is a messy eater. He got strawberry juice all over his snout, and his eyelashes. "You're a pig," I told him. But my dragon didn't care. He just shrugged his wings and pointed at my red hands. Then

I told my dragon, "Be quiet."

When we ran out of strawberries, we moved on

to watermelons. There's a watermelon tree in my

backyard. I picked two that looked juicy, and my

dragon split them in half over his knee. Then we dug

in. I spat the seeds out but my dragon just swallowed

them. "You're not supposed to swallow them," I told

him, "because a watermelon tree might grow inside

your stomach." I thought he stuck his tongue out at

me, but no, a dragon's tongue is black like licorice.

This was green. It was a leaf. Then more leaves came

out of his mouth, then a branch. It was definitely a

tree.

"I told you so," I said.

My dragon looked nervous. He looked unsure.

"What do you think we should do?" I said.

My dragon shrugged his wings.

"Maybe ... we should just wait and see," I said.

My parents like to say that.

My dragon nodded. While we waited, the tree grew. It grew fast. By lunchtime, it was as big as me. I went inside for lunch, and when I came back out, there was a full-grown watermelon tree sticking out of my dragon's mouth. There were already little watermelons growing on it. I didn't want to stare, but I couldn't help it.

"Can you breathe okay?" I asked.

My dragon nodded.

I was glad. If your dragon chokes, he isn't much

good to you. That's a fact.

"Are you hungry?" I asked.

My dragon nodded again. Dragons are always

hungry. I picked some of the little watermelons, and

dropped them down his throat. He swallowed them

whole like vitamins.

I got an idea, so I went and fetched the clipper-

snippers from the garage. "I can probably cut the tree

down," I said, clicking the blades together.

My dragon shook his head fast and waved his

claws. Little watermelons fell all over the place.

"Wait — you want to keep the tree?"

My dragon nodded.

I couldn't believe it. He wouldn't be able to breathe fire anymore. He wouldn't be able to toast my marshmallows anymore. I was pretty disappointed. But I respected his decision.

The tree didn't grow after that, but it did get greener and thicker. Birds built a nest in it. When their eggs hatched, I peeked in at the baby birds. "They sure are ugly," I said. My dragon looked offended. I guess to him they were beautiful.

The summer got hotter and hotter. Nine or ten times a day I had to turn the water hose on, and stick it in my dragon's mouth. The only thing thirstier than a dragon is a watermelon tree. It was hard keeping up.

The fall was a bad time for my dragon. First, the birds flew away. Then the leaves started dropping off. My dragon panicked. I had to tell him this was all a normal part of tree life, and not to worry. That helped a little.

Things got better in the winter. A few weeks before Christmas, I decorated the tree for him. I even put a star on the top. My dragon thought that was great — even better than having leaves, or birds. He showed his Christmas tree off to all the other dragons. They looked so jealous.

In the spring, the leaves came back. The birds came back, and built a new nest. Everything happened all over again. My dragon was used to all the changes

now, so they didn't upset him.

It's weird when there's a tree growing in your

dragon. It took a while, but I'm finally used to it,

too. I miss our old games, but now we have new

games. Like teaching songs to the baby birds, and

watermelon bowling.

My dragon is definitely happy, and that's what

matters. After all, if your dragon isn't happy, he's

not much good to you. And that's a fact.

The End.

Max's Rainbow

by Amanda Hill

It had rained all day. The endless patter of rain drops started off softly but then grew louder and louder until it seemed like there was an army of drummers outside Max's window. Then it was silent. Max's ears buzzed with the quiet, and he sat up straighter. He ran to his window and looked outside. The gray clouds were rolling away and the sun was finally beginning to peek through and stream down to the ground. A beautiful rainbow arched across the sky.

The rainbow looked so close, Max's fingers itched to touch it. No one has ever been close enough to touch a rainbow, but that doesn't mean it's impossible. Max pulled his big floppy rain boots over his feet and up to his knees. He opened up the back door and looked out into his back yard. The smell of mud and flowers wafted in. Max trudged out the door, down the stairs, and toward the rainbow.

The mud beneath max's feet squelched and oozed, threatening to pull off his boots. There were puddles everywhere that seemed to call, "Max, come jump in me." Max was happy to do so. He was having so much fun he didn't see the rainbow sprouting out of the ground right in front of him. In fact, he walked right into it. Bonk!

"Ouch!" Max rubbed his forehead and then gasped. He had found the rainbow! Max circled around it. The light filtered down in a way that seemed to move and tremble. And yet, when Max reached his hand out to touch it, the rainbow was quite firm. In fact, it felt as strong as cement. Upon closer examination Max noticed stairs carved into the mysterious rainbow. They were narrow and close together, and seemed to go on and on forever.

That's funny, thought Max. I always thought a rainbow would be more like a slide. Max didn't know if he would ever be able to find another rainbow, so he decided to see where the steps led. He took one step and then another — carefully at first, but with more confidence each time. Soon he was bounding up the rainbow two, three steps at a time. Before he knew it, he was high above the ground. He couldn't help but look down. The view made his stomach twist and his mouth run dry. His house seemed like a little doll house, and the people and cars looked like tiny ants.

Max continued to climb. At first there was only silence, then whispering wind and birds. But now, Max heard clanging metal, shouting, and roaring. That didn't sound right. Max's knees began to tremble. The noises were getting louder, and he could hear people screaming, "Retreat! Retreat!"

"That's it. I'm going back down," Max said. But just as he was turning around a horse flew up to him.

It was a beautiful white horse with silver wings and bright blue eyes. It hovered in the air just in front of Max, whinnied, and nodded his head toward the commotion. Max stared for a few seconds before the horse whinnied and nodded again.

I think he wants me to ride him, thought Max.

It is a little scary to try and mount a flying horse in midair. Max reached one arm out as far as he could. His fingers stretched and stretched but only brushed the edge of the horse. Max leaned out a little farther and then a little farther more. But he lost his balance. His foot slipped and he began to fall toward the dollhouses and ant people. Luckily,

Max was able to wrap his fingers around the horse's

mane just in time. He swung a leg up over the horse,

situated himself in the supple leather saddle, and

snapped the reins.

"Let's go!" he shouted. The horse raced toward

the commotion. As it flew to the top of the rainbow,

Max saw a castle made out of fluffy white clouds.

In front of the castle was the cause of all the noise.

A dragon was attacking. Men in silver armor riding

brilliantly white horses flew all around the dragon,

carrying sparkling swords. But the dragon's green

scales glimmered in the bright sun like they were

made of metal. They were too hard to be pierced by

swords. It roared and spewed bright orange flames at the castle. A tower began to melt away.

That dragon is going to melt the entire cloud castle, thought Max. I have to help. He directed his horse toward the fighting. When he got close to the dragon, Max realized he was not wearing any armor and he didn't have a sword. What was he going to do? Max flew past the dragon's head. It saw him and roared a roar so loud it made Max's teeth chatter. Max knew the flames were coming next.

"We've got to get out of here," he shouted to his horse. The horse quickly shot toward the earth. But the dragon spotted Max and followed. As Max hurtled through the air, he felt the searing pain of hot, flames brush past his neck. He looked behind him

and saw the dragon closing in!

"It's getting awfully hot back here," yelled Max.

His horse galloped through the air a little faster.

Max looked down at the ground for somewhere to

hide. He saw a forest not much farther ahead. "Get

to that forest!" he called. The horse obeyed and

swooped below the dense green tree tops.

The dragon was too big to fly through the forest,

but that didn't stop him. He flew over the tops of

the trees, still following Max and blowing his thick,

orange flames, igniting a forest fire! What should

Max do? He didn't want the forest to burn down,

but he didn't want to get barbecued either. Max

darted out the side of the forest, but a thin column

of flames drove him back inside. Max kept up this

wobbly pattern until he saw the edge of the forest

and the shores of a crystal blue lake.

"There, to that lake!" Max instructed his horse.

The dragon blew a spout of flames that caught the

horse's tail on fire. The horse whinnied and his eyes

grew wide with horror, but he kept flying toward the

lake.

"Hurry! Dive into the water!" Max commanded.

The dragon followed, entering the lake in a

tremendous splash. The wave of water hit Max and

the horse and sent them rolling head over heels

toward the shore. They scurried up on to the sandy

beach.

The dragon stood up and towered over Max and the horse. He flapped his huge leathery wings, sending the sand spraying into Max's eyes. Max couldn't see where to run! The dragon took a deep breath and roared. Max waited to be burned to a crisp. Instead he got a refreshing shower.

Max stared up at the dragon in shock. The dragon seemed equally surprised by what had just come out of his mouth. The lake water must have put out the dragon's flames. Max heard shouting overhead and saw the knights from the cloud castle descending toward the lake. They threw a large net over the dragon and tied him up.

One of the knights walked over to Max and held out his hand. "That was really brave, young man. What's your name?"

"Uh, Max." The knight held Max's hand in a tight squeeze and vigorously shook his arm up and down.

"Is there any way we can repay you?" the night asked. "You can ask for anything you desire."

Max thought for a minute. Anything he wanted? He looked back at his flying horse, walked over to him, and patted his neck. The horse nuzzled Max's face. "Can I have him?" Max asked.

The knight nodded. "His previous owner didn't fare as well as you against the dragon. Take good care of him."

"I will," said Max. His heart felt like it was going to pound out of his chest.

The other knights shouted and waved. "Well, it's time for us to go," said the knight. "Thanks again." Then he turned and marched back to the dragon.

The smell of smoke rolled past Max's nose and burned his eyes— the forest was still burning! "Wait," he cried. "We've got to put the forest fire out!"

Max quickly mounted his horse and the knights mounted theirs. Together they lifted the dragon high into the air. The dragon roared and blasted water every which way— the perfect fire fighter. The knights carefully flew the dragon over the burning forest.

Soon, all that was left was a smoldering patch of black. New trees would grow back one day.

When Max saw his house down below he broke off from the pack of knights and hovered in the air. The knights and the dragon disappeared into the clouds. Max patted his new pet on the head.

"What should I call you?" he asked. "How about Cumulus?" The horse neighed and nodded his head. "Cumulus," said Max. "Let's go home."

And when they returned, the sky had completely cleared—except for the faint outline of Max's rainbow.

The End.

The Dragon Artist's Tale

by Cynthia Reeg

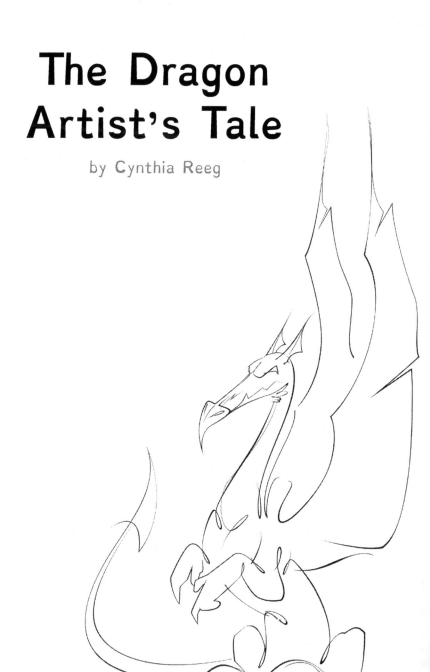

Rudy plopped onto the hard school bench.

"Welcome back, students, to Beginning Magicians Art Class." A smile creased Professor Bumbles' wrinkly face. Rudy had heard rumors that Professor Bumbles was the oldest teacher at Merlin Memorial Academy. More than five hundred-years-old.

"Today, students, we'll finish drawing our dragons for the school art contest."

Why couldn't the school have a Quickest Disappearing Act contest or a Magic Spell Olympics? Rudy might have a chance at winning one of those. Headmaster Ghouligan always said, "Magicians should be well-rounded in all areas of their education." Rudy sank down. He wished he could do his own disappearing act right now.

"Having a little trouble here?" asked Professor Bumbles. Rudy nodded. His drawing looked like a flabby toad.

"If you want to stay a few minutes after class today, we'll work on your dragon together," said Professor Bumbles. The end of class gong sounded. Rudy watched glumly as everyone nosily filed out. Everyone except him.

"Let's begin again." Professor Bumbles waved his magic wand. Rudy's toadish drawing vanished. "Now close your eyes. Picture your very own dragon."

Rudy closed his eyes. "All I can see is black."

"Try again," said Professor Bumbles with a wink.

Rudy took a deep breath and closed his eyes. He thought of bright dragon eyes. Sharp dragon teeth. A smoking dragon nose and a bumpy dragon tail.

"Whoa! I see it!"

"Good. Now keep your eyes on your dragon and let your fingers do the drawing."

Rudy touched his magic pencil to the paper. He imagined pointy dragon claws and giant dragon wings, and he kept his fingers drawing.

"That's it," said Professor Bumbles. You can draw. Wonderful, Rudy!" Clapping his hands, the ancient professor stumbled. His glasses fell to the floor, broken.

But Rudy hardly noticed the professor's problem.

Rudy was staring at his paper with his mouth wide open. There was the same dragon he'd pictured in his mind now on his paper. Rudolph Houdini Magus — the awful art student— had drawn a super dragon!

"Oh dear," said Professor Bumbles, fumbling through his pockets. "I think I have another pair of glasses here somewhere. And I know I have some paint you can use, Rudy. It's on my desk...or perhaps in my desk...."

Rudy reluctantly left his amazing dragon drawing to help search for the paint. Tugging on a heavy bottom drawer, Rudy nearly fell over as it creaked open. "Yikes!"

Lime-green lizards, magenta mice, and rainbow-colored bugs crawled in and out of the half-open

paint jars. When the colorful critters crawled back

into the paint, they disappeared!

"Ugh!" A purple frog hopped into Rudy's lap. "I

think I found the paint, Professor Bumbles." Rudy

tossed the slippery frog back into the drawer. Purple

paint now polka-dotted his pants.

Rudy spied a sealed paint jar in the far corner.

On the jar's lid, faded letters spelled "**DRAGON.**"

He grabbed the jar and slammed the drawer shut.

Professor Bumbles' squinty eyes studied Rudy's

find. "Yes, that's it...I think. Use that paint on your

dragon. Look at the picture in your mind as you paint.

Concentrate and let your fingers flow."

"Thanks," said Rudy, picking up his things. "I think this dragon is going to be something special."

Racing back to his room, Rudy put all the supplies on his desk. He opened the dragon paint carefully.

"Yuck!" What an awful smell! It stunk like rotten iguana eggs. Could magic paint go bad like spoiled goat's milk? Rudy shook his head. Now he was making excuses to keep from finishing the picture. What was he afraid of? The paint or himself?

Rudy picked up his brush and dipped it deep into the smelly paint. He would paint this dragon just as good as he'd drawn it. What did Headmaster Ghouligan always say? "A good magician is a confident magician. Believe in yourself and you can

create magic."

Rudy puffed out his chest. "I believe in me!"

He closed his eyes and imagined his dragon. Bright

yellow eyes. Deep red scales. Shiny white teeth.

Glowing green wings. And a blue-spotted tail. With

a steady hand, Rudy stroked the paint-filled brush

across the paper.

Yes! He was doing it. Rudy's dragon painting

looked unbelievably lifelike. He might have a chance

in the art contest after all. Rudy dipped the brush

again and held it above the dragon's claws.

"WHAT?" The dragon's eyes blinked at him! And

its blue-spotted tail thumped on the page! Something

had gone wrong. Maybe the professor's paint really

was rotten. Even as a junior wizard, Rudy knew

dragons were highly dangerous. He had to stop this

magic dragon mistake before it got any worse.

Rudy began pulling the brush back from the paper.

He wouldn't make the final stroke. And to be truly

safe, he should destroy the picture.

Rudy paused. If he destroyed this picture, would

anyone believe he'd created such a super dragon?

The dragon's green wings flapped menacingly on the

paper. Rudy shook his head. He must stop this dragon

now.

With a trembling hand, Rudy drew back the brush.

Oh no! The last drop of magic paint plopped onto the

paper. Rudy's dragon was complete!

Snorting steam, the dragon began inflating like a balloon. Puff by puff it grew bigger and bigger. In an instant Rudy's dragon was no longer flat, and it was no longer on the paper.

Rudy made a wild grab for his colorful dragon—now flying toward the open window. He clutched its blue-spotted tail. The dragon nearly wiggled from his hold as he tried to remember a spell. Rudy huffed. What was that spell he'd studied in Transformation Class? He could almost picture the textbook page it was on. Picture! Yes, now he remembered!

With a roar, the dragon twisted its head around toward Rudy.

"YIKES!" Rudy dodged a fiery shot and then with all his strength swung the still-growing dragon toward the ceiling and away from the open window. Another hot blast scorched Rudy's hair as he slammed shut the windowpanes. Ducking to the side, Rudy tumbled behind his desk.

Believe, Rudy thought. I gotta believe in me.

With a gulp, Rudy stood up. He held out his right hand as the dragon swooped toward him. "Dragon, dragon, beast too bold, become a picture to behold!"

A puff of fiery steam hissed from the magic dragon. Then with a choked cry it flew back onto Rudy's paper.

"Oh my, my, my," mumbled Professor Bumbles,

stumbling through the door. "I'm afraid I gave you the

wrong paint."

Rudy held up his magical dragon picture. "No

problem, Professor. I've got it all under control."

The professor pushed up his glasses on his bumpy

nose. "So I see."

Rudy beamed. "I believe my dragon will be the

most lifelike painting in the contest!"

Professor Bumbles smiled. "Without a doubt."

The End.

A Dragon in the Ice Cream

by Anne E. Johnson

"What should we do?" Kila asked as Anyi set her book bag down in the front hallway.

Anyi pretended to look for something in her bag. Kila was driving her crazy lately, but she didn't want to snarl at her so-called best friend.

"Well?" Kila had her hands on her hips, waiting for an answer.

"Let's have a snack," said Anyi, although she really wasn't hungry. She wondered why Kila could never think of what to do on her own.

Kila was already heading toward the kitchen. "What should we have?"

Why don't you decide? Anyi thought, but

she didn't say anything. While she searched the

cupboards for snacks, Anyi wondered what had

happen to their friendship.

"What are you in the mood for?" Kila's voice

sounded chipper. She seemed to think they were still

best friends.

Anyi sighed. "Let's have ice cream. I think there's

some left from my cousin's birthday party." She

was right. There was a big tub of ice cream in the

freezer. It should have been mostly empty, so Anyi

was surprised how heavy it was.

Kila was already sitting at the table, smiling

eagerly. Instead of smiling back, Anyi snapped, "You

could've gotten the bowls and spoons. You've been

here like a thousand times, so you know where they

are."

Kila shrugged and grinned again, so Anyi went to

the silverware drawer. Kneeling up on her chair, Kila

peered closely at the writing on the lid. "Why's this

ice cream called butter brickle?"

Anyi hesitated only for a second. Truthfully, she

didn't know why it was called butter brickle. But

Anyi couldn't stand to leave a question unanswered.

And she would never admit when she didn't know

something. "It's got those little brown specks in it."

She invented an answer as she went. "They're made

out of butter, and they're called brickles."

"Why are they called brickles? That's a weird

word."

If that girl asks one more question, Anyi thought,

I'm going to scream. But she made up an answer to

that one, too. "They look kind of like tiny bricks."

Before Kila could wonder about anything else, Anyi

ripped the wide lid off the tub of ice cream.

As she turned to place it on the counter behind

her, she could not believe what Kila said next.

"What's in the tub?"

Anyi spun around, shouting, "It's ice cream!

What's wrong with you? Don't you know anything?"

Kila's eyes were wide and her mouth hung open.

However, she didn't look like she'd even heard Anyi's

rude comments. She was still staring into the tub. "Is

that a dragon?"

It was such a strange question that Anyi couldn't help being curious. She peeked over the edge of the ice cream bucket.

No doubt about it, there was a little blue dragon in the ice cream. It had nestled waist-deep into the vanilla specked with crunchy candy. Its little blue snout pointed up at them and it paddled and slapped its front legs like it was playing in a mud puddle.

Gently, Anyi tipped the bucket just enough to look at its clear plastic bottom. She could see the pointed end of a blue tail.

"Is it a baby?" Kila asked as they watched the scaly creature lick toffee off its front claws.

Automatically Anyi pretended she knew the

answer. "Yes."

"Are you sure it's not a lizard?" asked Kila.

Anyi wasn't sure, but she didn't want to admit

that. She took a closer look. The dragon wiggled

a little and Anyi got her answer. "He has to be a

dragon," she said confidently. "He's got wings." She

was pretty proud of herself for noticing that.

"How do you know it's a boy dragon?"

Anyi thought about saying it must be a boy

because it was blue. But then, blue was also her

favorite color, and she was a girl. Also, the dragon

could be blue from the cold. He was, after all, sitting

in a bucket of ice cream.

While Anyi consider her answer, the dragon stretched out his tiny claws. He scooped his fingers deep into the ice cream and popped a frosty vanilla ball into his mouth.

"His talons," said Anyi. She'd learned that word from her older brother, who loved video games with dragons in them.

"His what?"

"His little clawed fingers," she said, holding up her own hand.

Kila narrowed her eyes. "What do the talons have to do with whether it's a boy? Wouldn't girl dragons have talons, too?"

The dragon made a funny swooping sound, like a

cow with its tail caught in a fence. He even seemed

to look at Anyi cockeyed, as if even he didn't think

his talons made him a boy.

Anyi knew she'd better make up something good.

"Boy dragons have longer talons than girl dragons."

Kila twisted up her mouth, clearly finding

something fishy with this answer. "Talons, huh?" She

appeared to think very hard before asking yet another

question. "Why's he in the ice cream?" Anyi heard a

note of challenge in her voice.

"Dragon's love ice cream," Anyi said as if it

were the most obvious thing in the world. "Can you

blame him? Wouldn't you like to crawl around in a

dessert?" The little blue dragon made a contented

cooing sound and licked his talons again. "See? He's

happy."

"Isn't it awfully cold in there, though?" Kila

moved her index finger slowly toward the dragon's

back.

Anyi was ready with an answer for that one.

"Dragons have fire inside them, so he stays warm."

She was glad Kila didn't ask why the ice cream didn't

melt.

"Can I touch him?"

Before Anyi could say "You'd better not," Kila

placed her finger right between the dragon's wings.

Anyi, who had seen some pretty scary dragons in her

brother's video games, closed her eyes for a second.

When Kila didn't scream, Anyi opened one eye. She couldn't believe what she saw.

The little dragon had his talons around the end of Kila's finger. Far from growling or biting, the dragon sounded like he was giggling. He squirmed around in the ice cream until his tummy was free from the chilly mound. Then he looked up at Kila with pleading eyes.

Anyi waited for Kila to ask what she should do. But Kila didn't ask. She went right ahead and gave that dragon a belly rub.

Surprised and a little annoyed, Anyi tried to take control. "Actually, I don't think it's a dragon after all. It's not magic or anything. If it were a dragon, it would be more magical. It's probably just a gross lizard that somehow got into our ice cream. You shouldn't touch it."

But Kila kept right on rubbing the dragon's belly, singing, "Pretty, pretty dragon, such a pretty dragon." While Anyi watched, jealousy crept into her heart. It was bad enough that Kila was deciding on her own what to do, but she also got to pet the dragon!

Anyi was about to shout at Kila, to call her a greedy creep, maybe even throw her out of the house. But just then Anyi and the dragon locked gazes. Its tongue was still busy cleaning ice cream off its talons, but Anyi swore she could hear a little voice in the back of her head, saying, "Ask Kila a question."

There was an impish gleam in that dragon's eye while it sighed and snuffled, wriggling happily under Kila's finger.

A question? Anyi thought. What would I ever need to ask Kila? Finally she thought of something Kila knew and she didn't. "What does dragon skin feel like?"

Instead of giving a know-it-all answer like Anyi was expecting, Kila smiled, pulled her hand out of the ice cream tub, and said, "You should find out for yourself."

So Anyi petted the dragon and was surprised all over again. If Kila had asked her earlier what a dragon belly felt like, she would have said "dry and scaly," pretending she already knew. But this dragon's tummy was soft and supple.

After a few minutes Kila took another turn at dragon petting (by this point he had turned over and was enjoying a back and wing rub). "I made that stuff up about dragons having fire inside them," Anyi admitted. "Do you think he's cold?"

"I don't know," Kila answered.

"You don't?" Anyi was disappointed for a second. But then she realized it was a very good answer because it gave them something to talk about. "He doesn't look cold," she said. "How do you think he stays warm in all that ice cream?"

"Well," Kila mused, furrowing her brow, "we

learned about warm blooded and cold blooded animals in school. Maybe dragons, since they're magical, have a whole different kind of blood, so they don't get too hot or too cold."

"Yeah, maybe," Anyi agreed. "Or maybe it's just worth being cold to be surrounded by ice cream!" She and Kila laughed at that, more than they'd laughed together in a long time.

Anyi noticed that she was starting to like Kila again and all because the dragon made her ask a question. She thought of one more thing to ask. "Did the dragon talk to you in your mind and tell you to rub its tummy?"

Kila looked at her like she was slightly nuts. "Of

course he didn't talk to me. I just figured he would

like getting his tummy rubbed." She giggled, "Don't

all creatures love that?"

"Yes, I guess they do." Anyi smiled at the dragon

who'd saved their friendship. He's magical after all.

The moment Anyi had that thought, the little blue

dragon spiraled up out of the ice cream and out

through an open window.

"That was incredible!" cried Kila.

"It sure was," Anyi agreed, thrilled to have her

best friend back. "What should we do now?"

"Well, we probably shouldn't eat that ice cream,"

Kila said decisively. "Let's have apples instead."

The End.

Princess Phoebe Finds a Job

by Debra Friedland Katz

Princess Phoebe sighed. Her tea had grown cold

and she had barely touched her crumpets. Her two

sisters, Princess Irene and Princess Marion, were

helping themselves to seconds.

"What's wrong?" asked Princess Marion.

"I'm bored," said Princess Phoebe. "I want something to do."

"I know what we can do," said Princess Marion. She plucked a strawberry from a bowl and popped it into her mouth. "Let's have a costume ball."

"That's not what I mean," said Princess Phoebe. "I want a job. And don't talk with your mouth full," she added. "It's rude."

"A job?" said Princess Irene. "A princess doesn't do anything — except tell other people what to do." She rested her feet on the table and leaned back in her chair. "I think a costume ball is a splendid idea."

"Please take your feet off the table," said

Princess Phoebe. "That's not a lady like way to sit."

Princess Irene placed her feet on the floor.

"We must get busy if we're going to have a costume ball," said Princess Marion. "We'll have to see to the invitations, and the costumes, and the food."

"The ballroom needs a new coat of paint," chimed Princess Irene. "And we need to order more chairs."

More chairs? That might be something she could do.

The next morning Princess Phoebe went to see the carpenter.

"I've already spoken to your sisters, and I've started on the chairs," said the carpenter.

"Wonderful," said the Princess. "I'm here to help build them."

"But...but...of course," sputtered the carpenter, who was not in the habit of arguing with a princess.

The carpenter showed Princess Phoebe the tools and explained how to use them.

Princess Phoebe set to work. The hammer was heavier than it looked, and she narrowly missed cutting her fingers with the saw.

When Princess Irene and Princess Marion came to check on the carpenter's progress, they were surprised to find their sister kneeling beside a chair, a hammer in one hand and a nail in the other.

"Can I sit in it?" asked Princess Marion.

"It's 'May I'," said Princess Phoebe, "and yes, you may."

Princess Marion perched gingerly on the seat. "It wiggles."

"I know," sighed Princess Phoebe. She laid the hammer and nail on the work bench and thanked the carpenter for letting her help.

The next morning Princess Phoebe called on the seamstresses.

"If you're here about the ball gowns," said the head seamstress, "your sisters have already ordered three."

"I'm here to help make them," said Princess Phoebe.

"Well...I...certainly," stammered the seamstress, who would never think to argue with a princess. She showed Princess Phoebe how to thread a needle, handed her two pieces of fabric, and showed her where to begin.

Later that day Princess Irene and Princess Marion stopped in the sewing room to see how their new gowns were coming along. They were again surprised to find their sister. She had a bunch of fabric in her lap and a needle and thread in one hand.

Princess Phoebe held up the dress she had been working on.

"I'm not wearing that one," said Princess Irene.

"If you can't say something nice, don't say it

at all," said Princess Phoebe. She put the gown on the table and thanked the seamstresses for their patience.

The next morning Princess Phoebe stopped in the castle kitchen.

"It's too soon to start on the food for the ball," said the head cook. "But we will be making cakes for afternoon tea.

Princess Phoebe lifted an apron off the hook on the wall and tied it around her waist. "I'd like to help."

"Help?" repeated the cook. "Well...if you insist." The cook gave the Princess a bowl and mixing spoon.

"Where's the recipe?" asked the Princess.

"Up here," replied the cook, tapping her head.

She recited the recipe for the Princess.

Princess Phoebe set to work. But she couldn't remember if the cake called for two cups of flour or three. She dropped egg shells in the batter and confused the salt with the sugar.

That afternoon Princess Irene and Princess Marion paid a visit to the kitchen. They were no longer surprised to find their sister, as her search for a job was the talk of the castle. On the table in front of her was a small cake.

"May I taste it?" asked Princess Marion. She tucked a napkin under her collar and picked up a fork.

"A napkin belongs on your lap," said Princess

Phoebe, "and yes, you may."

Princess Marion put her napkin on her lap and took a bite of the cake. She made a face.

Princess Phoebe untied the apron, laid it next to the cake, and thanked the cooks for allowing her into their kitchen.

Princess Phoebe knew there had to be something she could do.

She tried helping the scribe, but a day of writing invitations and addressing envelopes left her with a cramp in her hand.

She tried helping the royal gardener, but she couldn't seem to remember which end was up when planting the tulip bulbs, and she cut her dress with the hedge clippers.

She even tried helping the painters paint the ballroom, but standing on the ladder made her dizzy.

"You're not still looking for a job, are you?" asked Princess Marion one afternoon. The sisters were in the drawing room going through the day's mail.

"I..." began Princess Phoebe.

"It's here," exclaimed Princess Irene. "A response from Prince Henry." She tore open the envelope.

"It's not polite to interrupt," said Princess Phoebe.

"Sorry," said Princess Irene. She looked down at the envelope in her hands. She noticed a hang nail, which she began to chew.

Princess Phoebe had an idea.

On the morning of the ball Princess Irene and

Princess Marion sat in the drawing room discussing

last minute preparations.

"Where have you been all week?" asked Princess

Irene when Princess Phoebe appeared in the doorway.

"I've found a job," replied a beaming Princess

Phoebe. "Follow me. I'll show you."

Princess Phoebe led her sisters out of the castle

and across the moat to a small building.

"Isn't that the shed where the knights store their

old armor?" asked Princess Irene. "It looks different."

"It is different," said Princess Phoebe. The

armor was gone and replaced by tables and chairs constructed by the carpenter. The painters had given the walls a fresh coat of paint. The seamstresses had sewn curtains for the windows, and the gardeners had planted flowers next to the door.

Princess Phoebe pointed to a sign, hand lettered by the scribe, that hung above the door.

Princess Phoebe's Charm School

Manners Taught

Behavior Refined

"You were right," said Princess Phoebe. "A princess's job is telling other people what to do."

The End.

Register:

Register on our website (www.knowonder.com/register) to get **FREE** access to over 500 orignal stories, education tools and other resources to help you give the gift of literacy to your child, each and every day.

About Us:

Knowonder is a leading publisher of engaging, daily content that drives literacy; the most important factor in a child's success.

Parents and educators use Knowonder tools and content to promote reading, creativity, and thinking skills in children from zero to twelve.

Knowonder's Literacy Program – delivered through storybook collections – delivers original, compelling new stories every day, creating an opportunity for parents to connect to their children in ways that significantly improve their children's success.

Ultimately, Knowonder's mission is to eradicate illiteracy and improve education success through content that is affordable, accessible, and effective.

Learn more at

www.knowonder.com